NASA Takes Photography

INTO SPACE

by Arnold Ringstad

Content Consultant

Jennifer Levasseur, PhD
Museum Curator
Department of Space History, National Air and Space Museum
Smithsonian Institution

DEFINING IMAGES

Essential Library

An Imprint of Abdo Publishing | abdopublishing.com

abdopublishing.com

Published by Abdo Publishing, a division of ABDO, PO Box 398166, Minneapolis, Minnesota 55439. Copyright © 2018 by Abdo Consulting Group, Inc. International copyrights reserved in all countries. No part of this book may be reproduced in any form without written permission from the publisher. Essential Library™ is a trademark and logo of Abdo Publishing.

Printed in the United States of America, North Mankato, Minnesota
042017
092017

THIS BOOK CONTAINS
RECYCLED MATERIALS

Cover Photo: NASA
Interior Photos: JSC/NASA, 4, 6, 9, 12–13, 14, 27, 33, 35, 37, 38–39, 40, 58, 60–61, 65, 66, 100 (top middle); MSFC/NASA, 8, 28, 70, 98–99; US Army/NASA, 17; White Sands Missile Range/Applied Physics Laboratory/US Army, 18–19, 100 (top left); NASA, 23, 31 (left), 43, 63, 68–69, 72, 73; NASA/LOIRP, 31 (right); John Glenn/JSC/NASA, 24–25; ARC/NASA, 44; JPL/NASA, 46–47, 49, 51 (left), 51 (right), 53, 54–55, 56, 100 (top right); NASA/ESA/Hubble Heritage Team (STScI/AURA)/J. Hester, P. Scowen (Arizona State U.), 75, 100 (bottom left); NASA/ESA/G. Illingworth, D. Magee, and P. Oesch/University of California, Santa Cruz/R. Bouwens, Leiden University/HUDF09 Team, 76; NASA/JPL-Caltech, 78–79, 83; JPL-Caltech/Cornell/USGS/NASA, 80; NASA/JPL-Caltech/Univ. of Arizona, 82; NASA/JPL-Caltech/MSSS, 85, 87, 100 (bottom middle); ESA/NASA/JPL/University of Arizona, 88; NASA/JPL-Caltech/SSI, 90–91; NASA/JPL/ESA/University of Arizona, 93; Johns Hopkins University Applied Physics Laboratory/Southwest Research Institute/NASA, 94–95, 96, 100 (bottom right)

Editor: Melissa York
Series Designer: Becky Daum

Publisher's Cataloging-in-Publication Data

Names: Ringstad, Arnold, author.
Title: NASA takes photography into space / by Arnold Ringstad.
Description: Minneapolis, MN : Abdo Publishing, 2018. | Series: Defining images | Includes bibliographical references and index.
Identifiers: LCCN 2016962121 | ISBN 9781532110177 (lib. bdg.) | ISBN 9781680788020 (ebook)
Subjects: LCSH: Space photography--Juvenile literature. | Astronomical photography--Juvenile literature. | Outer space--Pictorial works--Juvenile literature. | Earth (Planet)--Photographs from space--Juvenile literature. | Photographers--United States--Juvenile literature.
Classification: DDC 520--dc23
LC record available at http://lccn.loc.gov/2016962121

CONTENTS

CHAPTER ONE

Earthrise

On Christmas Eve, 1968, three astronauts floated freely in their cone-shaped spacecraft. Commander Frank Borman, lunar module pilot William Anders, and command module pilot James Lovell could see the gray, pockmarked face of the moon below them. Their mission, Apollo 8, was tasked with orbiting 70 miles (110 km) from the lunar surface. It was one step in a long process of testing and proving the gear and procedures that would eventually land humans on the moon during the Apollo 11 mission. But for now, the Apollo 8 astronauts simply gazed down at the moon as they circled it.

As they rounded the edge of the moon on their fourth orbit, an incredible sight caught their eyes. Rising from behind the

The Apollo 8 crew, *left to right*, James Lovell, William A. Anders, and Frank Borman, were the first people to orbit the moon.

Earth is shown tipped on its side in the *Earthrise* photo. Antarctica is the white area to the left; the sunlight boundary crosses Africa.

lunar horizon was a brilliant blue-and-white marble: Earth. The cabin of the spacecraft filled with excited voices as the astronauts scrambled to grab their cameras.

Borman exclaimed, "Oh my God! Look at that picture over there! Here's the Earth coming up. Wow, that is pretty!" With Earth rising quickly, Borman and Anders asked Lovell to pass them rolls of color film. Lovell caught a view of his home planet, too, saying, "Oh man, that's great! Take several of them!"[1] He reached for another camera and began snapping away. One of Anders's shots would become one of history's most famous photos: *Earthrise*.

Borman later remembered how he felt the instant he saw the incredible sight out the window of the spacecraft:

> *I happened to glance out of one of the still-clear windows just at the moment the Earth appeared over the lunar horizon. It was the most beautiful, heart-catching sight of my life, one that sent a torrent of nostalgia, of sheer homesickness, surging through me. It was the only thing in space that had any color to it. Everything else was either black or white, but not the Earth.[2]*

Three days later, the command module streaked into Earth's atmosphere at more than 24,000 miles per hour (38,600 kmh). After shedding most of this speed through air resistance during its descent, it parachuted to a soft landing in the Pacific Ocean. The aircraft

CAMERA EQUIPMENT ON APOLLO 8

The Apollo 8 mission carried two Hasselblad EL cameras. These models were outfitted with electric motors that automatically wound the film to the next frame after a shot, saving the astronauts valuable time. The astronauts had three lenses for the cameras, two regular lenses and one telephoto lens that could take close-up photos of distant objects. Also included were seven magazines, or self-contained rolls of film. Three were black-and-white film, and four were color. The color magazines could shoot 160 photos each, and the black-and-white ones could shoot 200.[3]

The Apollo 8 capsule was recovered on December 27, 1968.

carrier USS *Yorktown* picked up the astronauts, and they returned to the United States. So, too, did their film.

Earthrise Returns to Earth

At the Manned Spaceflight Center in Houston, Texas, Apollo photography director Richard Underwood was responsible for processing the images. In a time long before digital cameras became mainstream, film had to be treated with chemicals in order to produce usable photographs. When the rolls of film from Apollo 8 arrived in Houston, the original negatives were immediately copied and placed into a secure vault as backups. Then, the lab began turning the raw negatives into finished photographs.

Before the mission, Underwood had foreseen the importance of a photo of Earth rising over the lunar horizon: "I argued hard for a shot of Earthrise, and we had impressed upon the astronauts that we definitely wanted it."[4] As soon as he saw the processed photo, he knew he had been right: "When I actually saw the picture, after they returned it, it was even better than I had anticipated."[5]

Underwood wasn't the only one to recognize the photo's significance. Of the hundreds of photos shot on Apollo 8, *Earthrise* drew by far the most attention. The image was soon featured in both *Time* and *Life* magazines, two of the biggest publications tracking the progress of 1960s space exploration. Upon the astronauts' return, the crew brought a framed print of *Earthrise* to President Lyndon B. Johnson. Newspaper editorials reflected upon the photo's connections to religion, international conflict, and humanity's place in the universe. The picture, showing Earth as a small, fragile, and uniquely habitable corner of the universe, became a potent symbol of the environmental movement. Decades later, Vice President Al Gore's Oscar-winning documentary about climate change, *An Inconvenient Truth*, used *Earthrise* as one of its central images.

RICHARD UNDERWOOD (1927–2011)

Richard Underwood, who led the team that modified cameras and trained astronauts for the Apollo Program, began his government career in the US Navy during World War II (1939–1945). After the war, he volunteered as an observer and photographer for atomic bomb tests. He went on to study aerial photography and worked for the US Army Corps of Engineers. He joined NASA in the early 1960s, and he quickly put his talents to work interfacing between the astronauts and NASA's photo labs.

Photographing the Frontiers of Space

The continued resonance of *Earthrise*, decades after it was taken in orbit around the moon, speaks to the power of space photography. Since its founding in 1958, the National Aeronautics and Space Administration (NASA) has documented its missions and gathered engineering data using cameras. These photographs have also served the twin goals of scientific discovery and public outreach. Scientists can study space photographs to learn more about planetary geology, the clouds of the gas giants, the nature of stars and galaxies, and humanity's influence on Earth. The public can see these images to appreciate the ingenuity of engineers, the daring of astronauts, and the beauty of the universe.

Taking photographs in space presents unique challenges. High radiation levels, extremely high and low temperatures, and the vacuum of space demand careful engineering in the camera hardware. For human missions, camera mechanisms must be designed so an astronaut in a bulky pressure suit can accurately aim and shoot. And after photos are taken, they must sometimes be transmitted millions of miles back to Earth. The development of digital camera technology was spurred by this need for easily transmitted photos.

The history of NASA itself can be traced through the agency's most significant images. In the 1960s, astronauts brought cameras to the surface of the moon. In the 1970s, robotic probes sent back photographs from Earth's neighbors in the solar system. The focus turned to Earth itself as the space shuttle gave astronauts an incredible viewing platform in orbit in the 1980s.

The 1990s brought the launch of the Hubble Space Telescope, providing the sharpest views

yet of deep space. And in the 2000s, the images sent back by next-generation space probes

gave scientists a better understanding of Mars and the outer solar system. At the same time,

astronauts mastered photography in low Earth orbit aboard the International Space Station

(ISS), an orbiting laboratory that allows astronauts to spend months in space. Through NASA's

photos, people around the world have been able to participate in some of the most amazing

voyages in human history.

CHAPTER TWO

Space Comes into Focus

The lights of Earth's cities are visible from space at night, as seen from the International Space Station, July 19, 2013.

The idea of viewing Earth from space has been the subject of speculation for thousands of years. The Roman philosopher Cicero pondered the idea in the first century BCE. In one of his writings, the general Scipio is magically whisked high enough into the air to see the entire planet at once. He remarks, "The Earth seemed to me so small that I was scornful of our empire, which covers only a single point, as it were, on its surface."[1] In the first-century CE writings of the Syrian author Lucian, a character who takes a similar journey recalls, "I was especially inclined to laugh at the people who quarreled about boundary lines. . . . The cities with their population resembled nothing so much as ant-hills."[2] The notion of such a view changing a person's perspective on life would remain a common theme into the modern space age.

Other writers speculated on how the planet would actually look from afar. In the 300s BCE, the Greek philosopher Plato described Earth as a brilliant, multicolored sphere, glistening in purple, gold, and white hues. Over the following centuries, other thinkers put forward their own views. In the 1600s CE, mathematician Carolus Malapertius theorized, "If wee were placed in the Moone, and from thence beheld this our Earth, it would appear unto us very bright, like one of the nobler Planets."[3]

The Age of Rockets

By the 1940s, technology was maturing to the point where viewing Earth from a rocket in space could soon be a reality. Rocket science had advanced by leaps and bounds during World War II (1939–1945). German dictator Adolf Hitler poured vast resources into programs that would use bomb-tipped rockets as weapons against his enemies. Leading his rocket program was German engineer Wernher von Braun. Approximately 4,000 of Braun's V-2 rockets rained down on the United Kingdom, Belgium, and other targets, killing thousands of civilians.[4]

A rocket attached to a V-2 missile base took off from Cape Canaveral, Florida, in 1950, the first launch of many from that site.

Germany's enemies, including the United States and the Soviet Union, recognized that the German rocket developments far outpaced their own. After the German surrender in May 1945, both nations worked quickly to gain control of both scientists and rocket hardware. The race was one of the first competitions of the Cold War (1947–1991), the period following World War II when the United States and the Soviet Union competed in ideological, economic, and technological ways without entering armed conflict against each other directly. The US forces got to Braun first, taking him, many other scientists, and more than 60 V-2s back to the United States. The German engineer would eventually take a leading role in

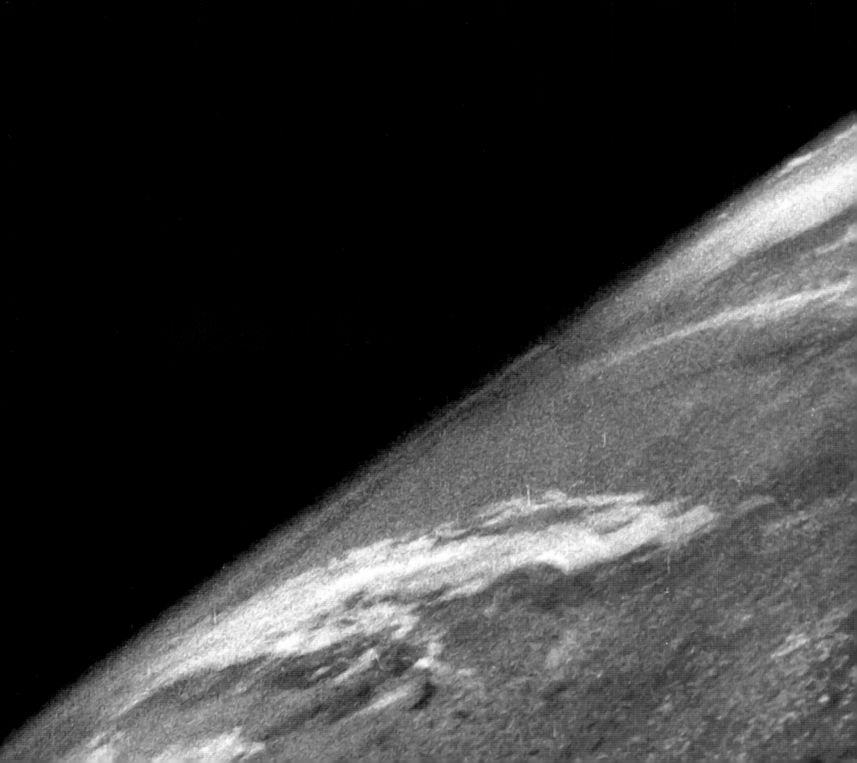

One of the first photos taken from space, from a V-2 rocket launched on October 24, 1946

the US space program, and the V-2 rockets would be taken apart, studied, and test launched. It was during these launches that the first photographs from space were taken.

Tests of the captured V-2s began in the New Mexico desert in the summer of 1946. Placing cameras in the rockets would make it possible to record their orientation and position in the atmosphere. There was relatively little interest in other uses for space photography at that time. When planning for rocket-based photography, the engineers soon discovered it presented several challenges. Cameras contain delicate parts, including film, springs, and shutters. To produce good photos, these parts must be able to withstand the trauma of a rocket launch and the subsequent descent back to Earth. In October, the team made the first attempt at a space photo, launching a V-2 with a 35-mm film camera to a height of 65 miles (105 km). After being fired straight up, the rocket fell back to Earth at high speed. The camera was destroyed, but the film, contained

PREDICTING THE FUTURE OF SPACE PHOTOGRAPHY

Following the successes of the V-2 photography, the project's camera engineer, Clyde Holliday, speculated on the potential future applications of photos taken from space. He predicted the eventual importance of reconnaissance and weather satellites:

> Results of these tests now are pointing to a time when cameras may be mounted on guided missiles for scouting enemy territory in war, mapping inaccessible regions of the earth in peacetime, and even photographing cloud formations, storm fronts, and overcast areas over an entire continent in a few hours.[5]

19

in a sturdy steel canister, survived the trip. The blurry images were the first photos successfully taken from space.

After refining the equipment, the engineers carried out more tests over the next few years. Some of the best photos were taken in July 1948, when a camera snapped more than 200 images from a V-2 at an altitude of 60 miles (97 km). The team recovered the film and stitched the photos into a broad panorama showing Earth stretching across 2,700 miles (4,300 km). On one edge of the image was Wyoming; on the other was Mexico. It was the first photo in which the curvature of Earth could clearly be seen. Rockets launching essentially straight up and falling straight down continued taking photos into the 1950s. But in the late 1950s, engineers developed rockets that could launch not only high but also far, picking up enough horizontal speed to remain in a stable orbit high above the planet. The breakthrough would kick-start the space race and bring about a new era in space photography.

NASA Is Born

The Soviet Union launched history's first artificial satellite, *Sputnik*, into orbit on October 4, 1957. US leaders knew the Soviets had been working on rocket technology, but the Soviet success shocked many US citizens who saw the Soviets as technologically inferior. If Soviet rockets were advanced enough to put a satellite into orbit, people worried, they could also carry atomic weapons to US cities with little warning. The United States quickly made moves to catch up in the struggle for space superiority. The competition became known as the space race.

One of the first US actions in the race was to establish a central agency to coordinate civilian space research and development. Separate groups in the army and the air force handled military rocket development. The civilian agency was NASA, formed in part from the earlier National Advisory Committee for Aeronautics (NACA). Congress passed legislation authorizing NASA's creation in July 1958. NASA began putting plans into motion for both remote-controlled and human-piloted missions. The agency's first satellite with a camera, *Explorer VI*, launched in August 1959. Its equipment, intended mainly to study radiation rather than take photographs,

ARGUING FOR PHOTOGRAPHY

Early in the history of space flight, it was already becoming apparent that a tension existed between the photography team and the scientists and engineers. Some felt photography was of little importance compared to the scientific and engineering objectives of each mission. Within NASA, Underwood was a major force in favor of photography:

> I used to scream at the engineers in meetings . . . 'You're going to spend $50 billion on everything else, yet you don't want to spend $20,000 on cameras. . . . Without those pictures, we'll have no idea of what happened up there. You can load thousands of books with all this computer data about our trips to the Moon, shove them in a library, and no one will ever read one.'[6]

produced grainy images. The next month, another Soviet first made it clear which nation held the lead in the space race. The Soviet probe *Luna-3* reached the moon and swung around its far side, taking photos of features never before seen by human eyes. The achievement made space photography a political issue. During his 1960 campaign for president, John F. Kennedy cited the *Luna-3* mission as highlighting the lack of US leadership in space, reminding voters that "the first photograph of the far side of the Moon was made with a Soviet camera."[7]

Humans in Space

On April 12, 1961, Soviet cosmonaut Yuri Gagarin became the first person in space. NASA had missed out on another first, this one by less than a month. Alan Shepard launched into space on May 5 aboard a Mercury capsule, becoming the first American astronaut. With Shepard's 15-minute flight as the only US mission into space, President Kennedy boldly pledged that the nation would land an astronaut on the moon before the end of the decade. NASA's Mercury and Gemini programs would help the agency refine its spacecraft and procedures. They would lead up to Apollo, the lunar exploration program.

This *Explorer VI* image shows sunlight and cloud cover over the central Pacific Ocean.

Glenn took this photo of Earth during his
Mercury mission.

Early attempts at photography during NASA's human spaceflight programs were relatively simple. In his 1962 Mercury mission, astronaut John Glenn brought along a slightly modified $45 camera he purchased from a drugstore. Underwood recalled that at a time when NASA was still trying to figure out the basics of space flight, photography was low on the priority list: "There was a great deal of objection to carrying cameras, because cameras [were heavy] and cameras took up space."[8] Only the final two of the six Mercury astronauts were trained in photography. And even these two, Walter Schirra and Gordon Cooper, had only a shared three-hour training session.

Schirra began a space photography tradition when he brought a 70-mm Hasselblad camera on his flight. Cameras made by Hasselblad, a Swedish manufacturer, were modified for use in space and became standard pieces of equipment during the Gemini, Apollo, and space shuttle programs. During Gemini, NASA began taking photography more seriously. The agency started preparing photographic plans for each mission. These plans described potential photography targets for the astronauts. Additionally, astronauts spent more time training with the cameras, practicing focus and composition.

The Gemini flights produced some of the most stunning space photographs yet. On June 3, 1965, US astronaut Edward H. White III left his spacecraft for an extravehicular activity (EVA), or spacewalk. Later Gemini astronauts also performed EVAs, refining techniques that would be used on the lunar missions. With no windows between photographer and subject, the images astronauts took while performing EVAs were crystal-clear. Astronauts floated freely over the blue, white, and brown globe far below. NASA's photographs allowed the public to share this incredible view. Underwood noted, "We wanted pictures that recorded it the way the astronauts saw it."[9]

By the conclusion of Gemini in 1966, NASA had developed its skills in rendezvous and docking, the joining together of two spacecraft in orbit. It completed a successful long-duration space flight lasting two weeks. And it had shown astronauts could complete tasks during EVAs. All the pieces were in place for the Apollo missions to the moon. Each Apollo flight would carry only three astronauts, but space photography would allow billions on Earth to come along for the ride.

White performs an EVA, June 3, 1965.

CHAPTER THREE

Photos from the Moon

The *Ranger IV* launched into space on April 23, 1962, headed for the first US lunar impact.

Before NASA could safely send humans to the surface of the moon, it sent a series of robotic missions to learn more about the lunar environment. The first, the Ranger program, sent probes on a crash course with the moon, taking photos right up until they smashed into the surface. The later Surveyor program achieved soft landings, sending back data on the soil and landscape. Cameras on the Surveyor landers took astronaut's-eye-view photos of the surface. And the Lunar Orbiter probes circled the moon in 1966 and 1967, taking high-resolution photos in wide swaths and scouting out prospective landing locations for the Apollo missions.

Lunar Orbiter

Getting orbital imagery of the moon was critical for NASA's mission planners. But returning these images across approximately 240,000 miles (386,000 km) of space presented a major challenge. For the Lunar Orbiter program, NASA and the spacecraft's builder, aircraft company Boeing, developed a novel solution.

Inside each Lunar Orbiter probe would be a miniaturized photo processing lab. Traditional photo processing liquids could slosh around inside the spacecraft, so the engineers used a dry development process. After each black-and-white photo was taken and processed, the probe would electronically scan it and transmit the resulting data back as an electric signal. Sending a pair of photos took up to 45 minutes. Once the data was received by networks of antennae on Earth, it could then be put back together to create the images.

Apollo

In early 1967, NASA's team at the Kennedy Space Center on the Florida coast prepared to launch the first Apollo crew into orbit. Mercury and Gemini had achieved their critical objectives, and Apollo seemed poised to carry that momentum all the way to the moon. But on January 27, the

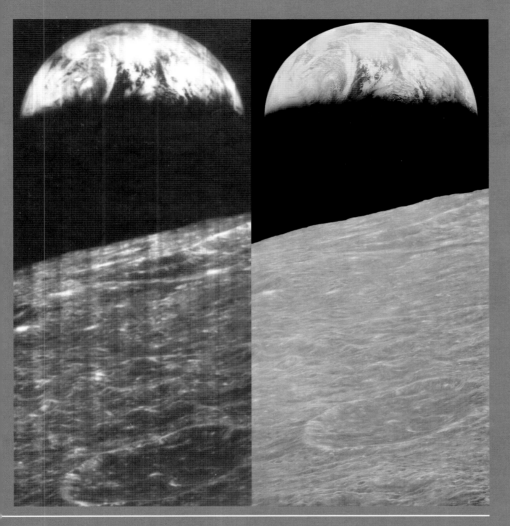

Original (left) and restored (right) versions of a Lunar Orbiter image of Earth and the moon

RECOVERING THE LUNAR ORBITER PHOTOS

The Lunar Orbiter photos were impressive when they were originally beamed back to Earth in the 1960s. But decades later, a team of engineers learned that by going back to the original data and using modern computer processing, they could create higher-quality images. Co-led by former NASA employee Keith Cowing and Dennis Wingo, president of an aerospace engineering company, the team behind the Lunar Orbiter Image Recovery Project (LOIRP) recovered the mission's original data tapes in 2005. They also gained access to the refrigerator-sized tape drives required to read the data.

The LOIRP team repaired the aging drives and learned how to retrieve and reassemble the data. They eventually recovered a famous shot of Earth rising from behind the moon, producing a dramatically improved version of the image. This convinced NASA to give the group official funding in 2008. It has continued its work, recovering hundreds more images from the Lunar Orbiter tapes. Cowing says, "We're reaching back to a capability that existed but couldn't be touched back when it was created. It's like having a DVD in 1966, you can't play it."[1]

program came to a tragic halt. During a routine ground test, astronauts Virgil I. "Gus" Grissom, Edward H. White III, and Roger Chaffee sat sealed in an Apollo command module. Suddenly, faulty wiring created a spark in the cockpit. The fire quickly grew to fill the spacecraft, feeding on the pure oxygen atmosphere inside. Unable to open the hatch and escape, the astronauts suffocated. The nation mourned the three men, and NASA oversaw a redesign of the command module that incorporated numerous safety improvements. With just a few years left before the end of the decade, the agency pushed ahead with the Apollo program.

The first crewed Apollo flight, Apollo 7, carried out a successful test of the redesigned command module in Earth orbit in October 1968. It was followed by the daring flight of Apollo 8 in December of that year and Apollo 9, a test of the lunar module in Earth orbit, in March 1969. The May 1969 Apollo 10 mission sent both modules to the moon for the first time, rehearsing everything but the lunar landing itself. That task would be up to Apollo 11, which prepared for liftoff in July.

Photography, especially on the lunar surface, would be the Apollo program's face to the public. The astronauts' time on the moon would be limited, and there would be no second

chances. To maximize the odds of successful shots, NASA stepped up its efforts in both camera hardware and photography training.

Preparing for the Moon

As with the other Apollo missions, the primary still cameras carried on Apollo 11 were Hasselblads. Two traveled down to the lunar surface with Neil Armstrong and Buzz Aldrin. A third remained in the command module with Michael Collins. Of the two cameras brought to the surface, one was designated the data camera. It had additional modifications, including a Reseau plate. This piece of transparent glass, placed between the film magazine and the body of the camera, was engraved with hash marks making up a grid. This grid appeared on each photo taken with the camera. Once the film from the camera was developed, the marks allowed accurate measures of distances and heights.

The lunar cameras also had modifications to make them easier to use for fully suited astronauts. Large, simplified controls made it possible to operate the camera while wearing bulky gloves. With a helmet on, an astronaut could not lift the camera to his face and look through a viewfinder. Instead, the astronauts trained to use their body position to roughly aim. Rather than twisting a ring to adjust the camera's focus, astronauts chose from three preselected focuses: near, medium, and far.

During training, astronauts went on trips during which geologists taught them how to identify, describe, and study various types of rock. They often brought along their cameras on these trips to practice their photography

LUNAR CONDITIONS

To survive and operate on the lunar surface, the astronauts' cameras had to be extremely rugged. NASA's requirements included:

- ⊙ Surviving the acceleration of launch and impact of landing.
- ⊙ Surviving air pressure changes ranging from sea level on Earth to the lunar vacuum.
- ⊙ Surviving temperatures ranging from −303 degrees Fahrenheit (−186°C) to 237 degrees Fahrenheit (114°C).[2]
- ⊙ Surviving high radiation.

skills, estimating by eye what the appropriate camera settings should be. The astronauts trained to use a technique called exposure bracketing when photographing particularly important subjects. An overexposed shot would have too much light, with the bright areas washed out. An underexposed shot would have too little light, rendering the subject dim or muddy. After taking a photo with the recommended exposure, they would take additional photos one stop above and below that setting, aiming to ensure at least one of the images would turn out well.

Neil Armstrong of Apollo 11 practices using a television camera in his bulky suit while still on Earth.

Photographing the First Landing

The work in hardware and training paid off. Armstrong and Aldrin landed in the lunar region known as the Sea of Tranquility on July 20, 1969. A few hours later, Armstrong and Aldrin exited the spacecraft and walked on the lunar surface. Aldrin took a handful of photos, but Armstrong was the primary photographer. While on the moon, Armstrong took hundreds of photos of their landing site, the lunar module, nearby rocks, Aldrin, and even a small, distant Earth. Some of these images are amongst the most iconic photographs in human history. One is a front-facing view of Aldrin standing on the lunar surface. Armstrong and the lunar module are visible in Aldrin's reflective visor. Another shot, taken by Aldrin, shows the astronaut's boot print in the moon's soil.

PHOTOS OF ARMSTRONG ON THE MOON

Nearly all of the Apollo 11 photos of an astronaut on the lunar surface depict Aldrin. Only a few shots show Armstrong, either in the distance or from behind. Why aren't there more photos of the first man on the moon? Armstrong, the primary photographer, carried the main camera and took most of the photographs.

The two astronauts lifted off from the moon on July 21, meeting up with Michael Collins in the command module in lunar orbit. From there, they returned to Earth, splashing down in the Pacific Ocean on July 24. NASA had fulfilled

Kennedy's pledge to land men on the moon and return them safely to Earth. Once the film was processed and copies were distributed to the media, the crew's historic photographs filled newspapers and magazines across the globe.

Five more successful landings followed. Another mission, Apollo 13, experienced an explosion on the way to the moon that forced the astronauts to return home without landing. With the crippled spacecraft suffering from limited supplies of water and power, the efforts of the engineers in Mission Control made it possible for the crew to get back to Earth safely.

Blue Marble

Apollo 17 was the final mission to the moon. Its crew, Eugene "Gene" Cernan, Harrison "Jack" Schmitt, and Ronald Evans, launched in December 1972. Their destination was the moon's Taurus-Littrow Valley. Along the way, they would take one of the most reproduced images ever.

Five hours after launch, one of the crew members, most likely Schmitt, looked out the window. He saw a fully illuminated Earth and took several photos, capturing what some now call the *Blue Marble* photo. When technicians back on Earth saw the image, they immediately recognized its importance. Underwood recalled, "More people have seen that photo than any in the history of mankind, and I saw it first. I was the first person to see that photograph. It was wet in a processor in Building 8. When I saw it I said, 'Boy, that's it.'"[3]

The *Blue Marble* photo shows Africa centered with the island of Madagascar to the right and Antarctica partially obscured by clouds below.

Apollo 17 was the first time a human being ever saw the completely lit disc of the planet. The timing of each Apollo mission was carefully planned to allow for ideal lighting conditions during landing. The angle of the sun had to be such that boulders and craters cast visible shadows, making them easier to see and avoid. The result of this, combined with the location of the landing sites, meant most Apollo astronauts would see only a shadowy crescent Earth. But the requirements for getting to Taurus-Littrow meant the Apollo 17 crew would have the chance to see a fully lit Earth. The crew took advantage of the opportunity, snapping an iconic photograph that later became synonymous with the environmental movement.

In 1973, extra Apollo hardware was used to launch the first US space station, Skylab. In 1975, an Apollo command module was put into service for a joint mission with the Soviet Union, meeting up with a Soviet Soyuz capsule in Earth orbit. It would be six more years before another American flew in space. But by this time, NASA had developed a robust program of robotic space probes. Throughout the 1970s, these robotic explorers went out into the solar system and sent back valuable data on the planets, including spectacular images of these faraway worlds.

Photographing the Apollo Landing Sites

Using Earth-based telescopes, it is impossible to see the objects left behind by the Apollo astronauts, including parts of the lunar modules. These things are too small, and the moon is too far away. However, a spacecraft orbiting the moon with a high-quality camera can see them. This is just what the Lunar Reconnaissance Orbiter (LRO), launched in June 2009, has done. The probe's main objective is to create detailed maps of the moon. This capability also gave it an opportunity to check in on the long-abandoned Apollo landing sites.

In 2011, the LRO maneuvered into an extremely low orbit around the moon, approaching as close as 13 miles (21 km) from the surface. Using a set of high-quality digital cameras, it returned incredible images showing lunar modules, equipment, and even footprints from the Apollo landing sites. Lunar geologist Noah Petro explains, "We can retrace the astronauts' steps with greater clarity to see where they took lunar samples."[4]

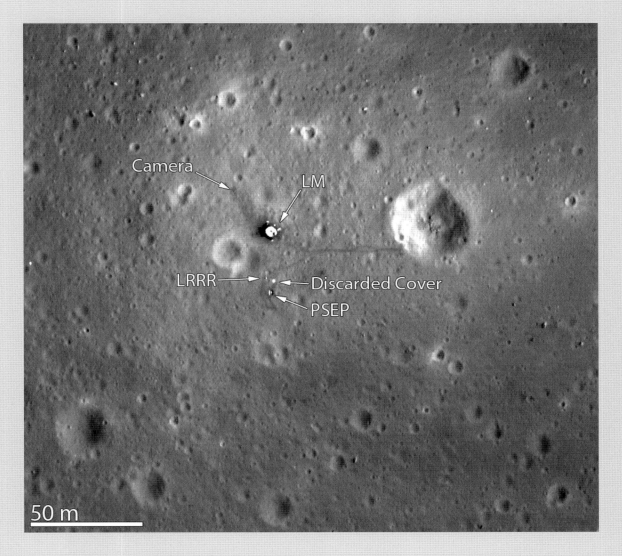

The LRO photographed the Apollo 11 site. Labeled are a camera, the lunar module (LM), the Passive Seismic Experiment Package (PSEP), which measured volcanic activity on the moon, the Laser Ranging RetroReflector (LRRR), which reflects a laser beam off mirrors to measure the distance between Earth and the moon and is still used today, and its discarded cover.

CHAPTER FOUR

Voyaging to the Planets

NASA's twin probes *Pioneer 10* and *Pioneer 11* were the first artificial objects to depart the inner solar system for the vast gas giant–dominated outer solar system. *Pioneer 10* launched in 1972, and *Pioneer 11* followed in 1973. The earlier probe flew only to Jupiter, while its counterpart visited both Jupiter and Saturn. The missions collected the first close-up photos of the solar system's two largest planets.

The Pioneer probes used an unusual camera type known as an imaging photopolarimeter. Rather than collecting all of the light from

Pioneer 10 image of Jupiter showing the planet's famous red spot, as well as the shadow of the moon Io. The image was enhanced from the raw data captured by the spacecraft.

a view at once, this instrument collected a single, very thin strip of an image at a time. Each strip covered only 0.03 degrees of the instrument's field of view. To create an image, the entire spacecraft spun around. With each revolution, a new strip was added to the picture. It took up to 30 minutes to take each photo. During the closest approaches to Jupiter and Saturn, when the spacecraft were moving fastest, the long duration of the process could result in blurring. Still, both probes were major successes, collecting impressive images in addition to the wide array of data gathered by their other instruments.

Landing on Mars

NASA's gaze turned back toward the inner solar system in 1975 when they sent two Viking spacecraft to Mars. Each included both a lander and an orbiter. Upon reaching Mars, the two parts split. The landers descended to the Martian surface, while the orbiters remained in orbit to observe the planet from above. The orbiters used antennae to relay data from the landers back to Earth. The main objective of the Viking program was to search for evidence of life, and the landers were equipped with multiple instruments to detect these clues. Each lander also had a camera attached to the top of its main structure. The panoramic camera scanned up,

down, and across to focus light on its sensor. It could generate images up to 512 pixels tall. The width of the photos depended on how far the camera scanned left to right.

The camera mechanism was designed with Martian conditions in mind. The planet's winds kick up dust that could potentially damage the delicate system. When it was not actively taking photos, the camera could be rotated behind part of the lander's structure to shield it from blowing dust. Additionally, if dust built up on the lens, a nozzle could spray pressurized carbon dioxide gas to clear it.

The *Viking* landers took approximately 6,600 photos over the course of their missions.[1] The images had multiple purposes. Geologists could use them to study the local rock formations. Mapmakers could use them to verify exactly where the landers set down. Meteorologists could use them to study the changes in the environment caused by Martian dust storms. And in the event that the other instruments detected signs of life, the cameras would be able to observe it firsthand. Though the Viking program taught scientists a great deal about Mars, it did not find any definitive evidence of life.

The Voyagers

Another pair of spacecraft, *Voyager 1* and *Voyager 2*, served as the flagship missions of NASA's solar system exploration program of the late 1970s. Both launched in 1977 and would be the most ambitious probes yet. *Voyager 1* would fly near Jupiter and Saturn, then swing past Saturn's moon, Titan, on its way out of the solar system. It eventually exited the solar system in 2012. *Voyager 2* would take advantage of a rare planetary alignment to visit Jupiter, Saturn, Uranus, and Neptune in a single mission.

The Face on Mars

As the *Viking* landers studied Mars at close range, the pair of orbiters continued circling the planet, taking photographs. One of the photos it sent back fueled conspiracy theories for decades. Taken by the *Viking 1* orbiter in 1976, the photo shows a landscape dotted with craters and mesas. One of the mesas appears extremely similar to a human face. Some people latched onto this photo as evidence of an ancient Martian civilization. Scientists responded by noting that a coincidental combination of light, shadow, and small black dots caused by errors in the data was simply creating the illusion of a face.

Still, when the Mars Global Surveyor (MGS) reached the red planet in 1997, scientists prepared to photograph the same mesa with the new probe's higher-quality cameras. When MGS took new photos in 1998 and again in 2001, it was clear the mesa was a natural landform. Under different lighting conditions and with a better camera, the illusion disappeared. The phenomenon was an example of pareidolia, seeing a pattern or meaning where none really exists. Scientists suggest that the human brain's ability to recognize faces and tendency to assemble visual input into understandable patterns may be responsible for this kind of illusion.

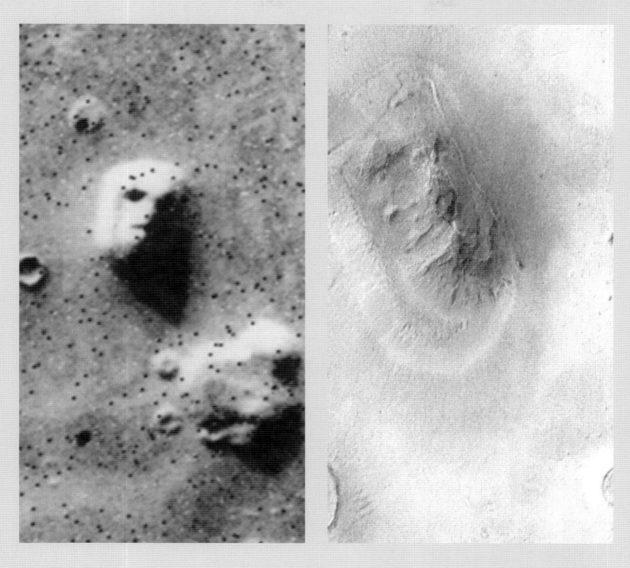

The Mars "face" and the later
photograph disproving the illusion

Both Voyagers were dramatic successes, beaming back the clearest photos yet of Jupiter and Saturn and the first-ever close-up shots of Uranus and Neptune. But the most famous photo of the program was taken after *Voyager 1* was well on its way out of the solar system.

Pale Blue Dot

Well-known planetary scientist Carl Sagan had been closely involved in the Voyager program. Years earlier, during the Apollo program, he had noticed that the *Blue Marble* photo of Earth had made national boundaries disappear. The image had given many people a new perspective on their relationship with the planet and with each other. Sagan now saw an opportunity to take another image that would emphasize Earth's small, fragile place in the cosmos.

Sagan came up with the idea of turning *Voyager 1* back toward Earth and taking a photo of the planet, now distant and faint. But some at NASA argued against the idea. Pointing the camera at Earth also meant pointing it toward the sun, risking damage to the lens. The Voyager team would have to wait until the mission's planned photographs were finished being taken. After a series of delays, Sagan discovered the team who sent radio commands to *Voyager 1* would soon be shut down. If the photo was going to be taken, it had to be done soon. Finally, NASA administrator Richard Truly intervened and ordered the photo to be taken.

Candy Hansen of the Jet Propulsion Laboratory and Carolyn Porco of the University of Arizona put the sequence of camera commands together. In February 1990, it was time to take the shot. As it sped away from the sun at 40,000 miles

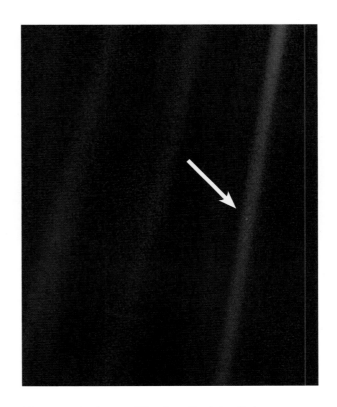

Voyager 1's photo of Earth, called the *Pale Blue Dot*

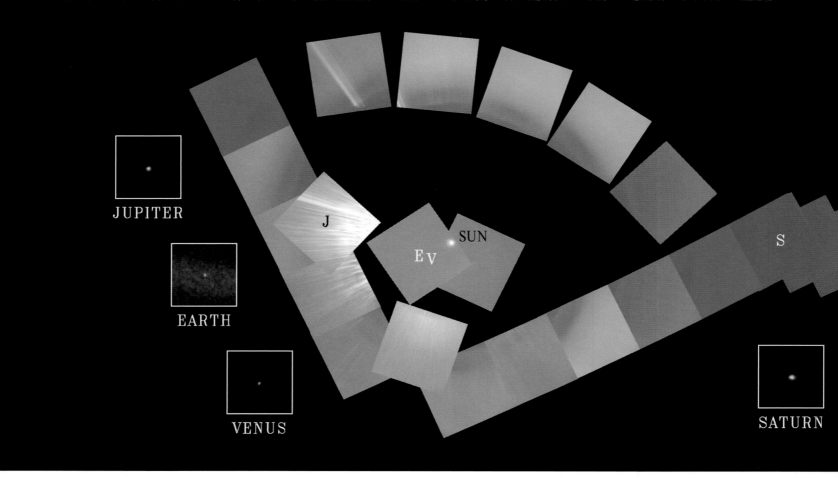

The *Voyager Family Portrait*

per hour (64,000 kmh), *Voyager 1* spun around, took a series of 60 photos, and transmitted them

back to Earth.[3] Technicians assembled the photos into a broad mosaic showing the sun, Venus,

Earth, Jupiter, Saturn, Uranus, and Neptune. The mosaic became known as the *Family Portrait*.

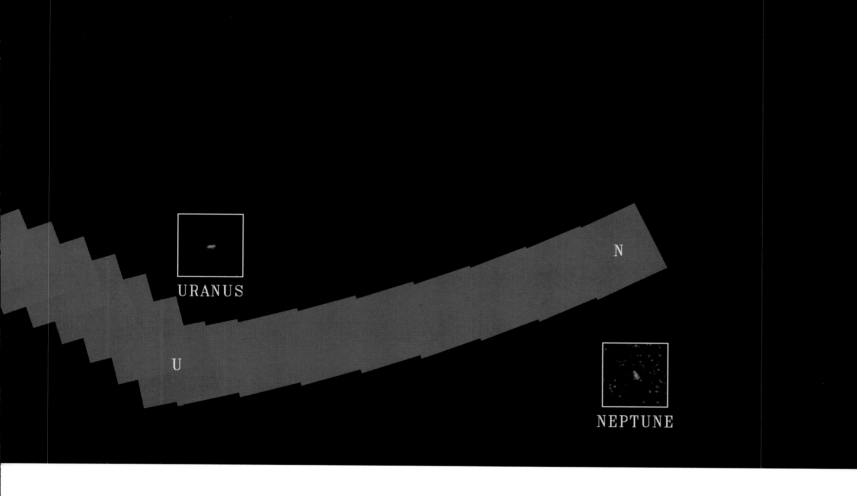

The image of Earth showed the planet as a tiny blue ball in a vast sea of blackness. Sagan

called it the *Pale Blue Dot* photo. He believed he and the Voyager team had succeeded in

capturing the important image he sought: "There is perhaps no better demonstration of the

Voyager 2's portrait
of Uranus

folly of human conceits than this distant image of our tiny world. To me, it underscores our responsibility to deal more kindly with one another, and to preserve and cherish the pale blue dot, the only home we've ever known."[4]

When the Voyager probes left Earth, intensive testing was already underway on NASA's next human spaceflight program. The new spacecraft looked wildly different from the earlier capsules. Soon, astronauts would be flying into space in a huge, airplane-shaped vehicle called the space shuttle. The shuttle, along with the space station it helped build, would allow astronauts to live in orbit for weeks at a time. They would be perfect vantage points for turning their cameras back toward Earth.

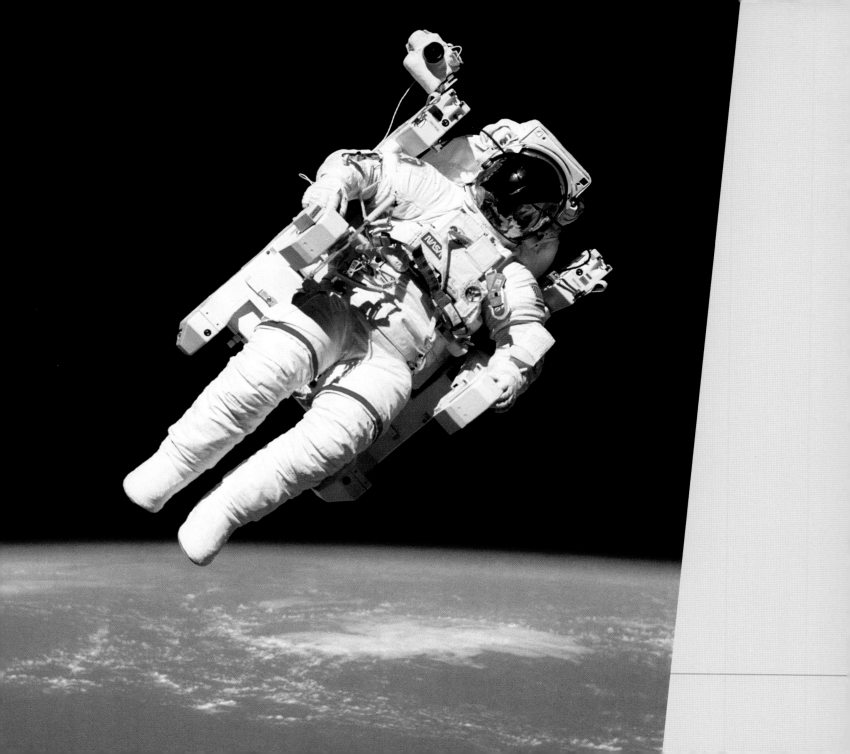

CHAPTER FIVE

Turning the Camera Back toward Earth

The first space shuttle mission, STS-1, launched in April 1981. Capable of carrying seven crew members and a large volume of cargo into Earth orbit, the shuttle made 135 trips into space over the next three decades.[1] The space shuttle could remain in orbit for more than two weeks at a time, giving astronauts plenty of time for taking pictures. Some took up photography as a hobby, continuing to shoot photos even during their personal relaxation time.

While on a space shuttle mission in 1984, astronaut Bruce McCandless performed the first untethered EVA.

For shuttle astronauts, the main photography subject was Earth. As space shuttles continued flying, the catalog of orbital photography expanded. The same places could be viewed and tracked over the course of years. The growth of cities was studied over time. Scientists traced how erosion shaped and reshaped waterways. They examined wide-scale damage to coral reefs and the spread of smog in urban areas.

Astronauts also used photographs to study the shuttle itself. The underside of each space shuttle was covered in thousands of heat-resistant tiles to protect the vehicle during the fiery process of reentry. As the shuttle descended back into the atmosphere for landing, the fast-moving vehicle collided with air molecules, generating extremely high temperatures. The tiles helped the shuttle deflect this heat and survive reentry. However, the tiles themselves were vulnerable to other types of damage, either during launch or while in orbit. A damaged tile could let heat through to the vehicle's structure, potentially causing a catastrophic accident. While still in orbit, shuttle astronauts on missions after 2005 used cameras at the end of a long robotic arm to inspect the vehicle's underside. They could check the heat shield's condition before returning to Earth.

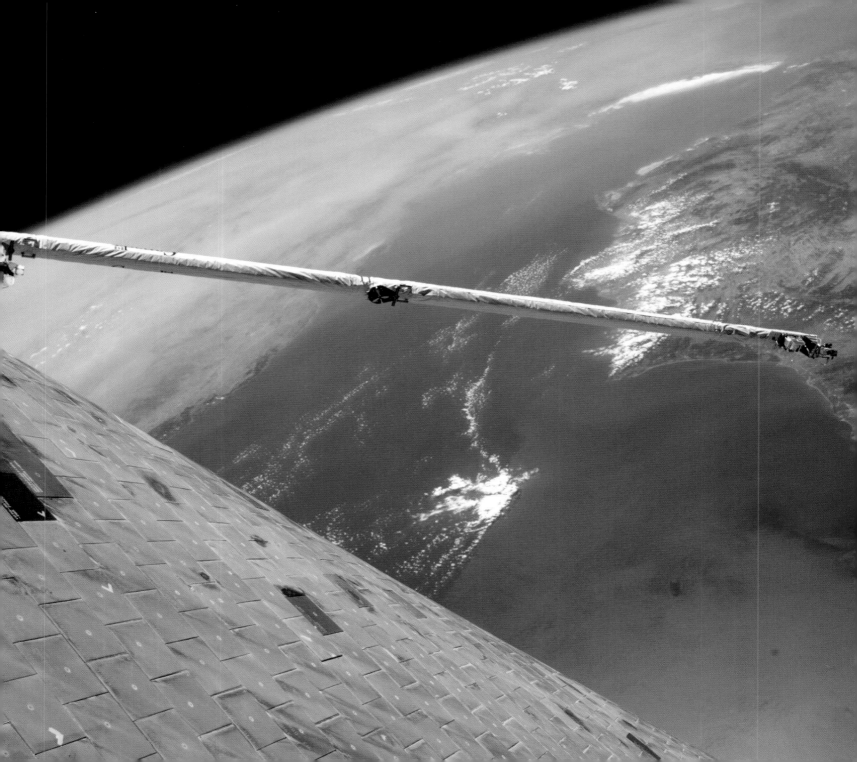

Disasters on Film

The space shuttle program experienced two major disasters during its 30-year run. In 1986, the shuttle *Challenger* broke apart 73 seconds after liftoff. And in 2003, the shuttle *Columbia* disintegrated while reentering the atmosphere. In both cases, photography played an important role in determining what went wrong.

Photos taken during the launch of *Challenger* showed what looked like gray smoke coming from one of the shuttle's solid rocket boosters (SRBs). The SRBs, two tall, white tubes on either side of the large orange fuel tank, help propel the shuttle upward during the early phases of launch. During *Challenger*'s launch, a rubber gasket inside the SRB was affected by the colder-than-normal launch weather and failed. The broken gasket led to the explosion of the SRB, destruction of the shuttle, and loss of all seven crew members. The small trail of smoke seen in launchpad images was one major indication of what went wrong.

During the *Columbia* launch, a camera caught a piece of foam insulation falling off the external fuel tank and striking one of the shuttle's wings. NASA had seen similar events happen before, but technicians did not consider the potentially catastrophic effects a large section hitting the vehicle at a high speed could have during reentry. When *Columbia* reentered the atmosphere, superheated gases entered a hole in the wing where the insulation had hit, leading to the breakup of the vehicle and loss of the crew.

Gray smoke at liftoff signaled the fatal damage to *Challenger*.

The International Space Station

One of the space shuttle's major tasks was to help assemble the International Space Station (ISS). This large orbiting outpost is jointly run by the United States and Russia. Several other countries also contributed to the project. A Russian rocket launched the first module for the station in November 1998. A few weeks later, the space shuttle *Endeavour* brought the second module and connected the two pieces together. Over the course of the next 13 years, more than 30 Russian and US shuttle missions added components to the ISS and delivered critical supplies.

Astronauts live on the ISS for months at a time, giving them ample time for both mission-related and personal photography. Among the most popular places for taking photos is the Cupola module, added to the station in 2010. The dome-shaped module, built by the European Space Agency, is shaped like a hexagon, featuring six windows around the sides

THE SALLY RIDE EARTHKAM

Sally Ride became the first US woman in space in 1983. After leaving NASA, she continued working in education and public outreach. One of her most notable projects was EarthKAM, standing for Earth Knowledge Acquired by Middle School Students. The program involved a laptop-controlled camera carried aboard the space shuttle and pointed down at Earth. Middle school students from around the country could put in requests to take images of specific places on the planet. In 2001, the camera was moved to a permanent home on the ISS. Following Ride's death in 2012, NASA renamed it the Sally Ride EarthKAM.

and one large, circular window in the middle. Up to eight cameras are kept ready for use in the Cupola.

Dmitry Kondratyev, *left*, and Paolo Nespoli photographing Earth from the ISS Cupola, 2011

By the early 2000s, digital photography had become a mature technology. NASA replaced film cameras with an array of digital ones. Digital photography carries many advantages over using traditional film. After taking a photo, the astronaut can simply send it electronically down to Earth. The switch to digital also meant the astronauts could take an unlimited number of photos without worrying about running out of film. The number of photos they shot increased dramatically. During a six-month stay on the ISS in 2010, the ISS crew took approximately 100,000 photos.[2]

INTO THE LENS

SOCIAL MEDIA

American astronaut Mike Massamino sent the first tweet from space in 2009. Since then, many astronauts have started social media accounts and send photos and video from the ISS. Social media is an optional part of the job, but many astronauts choose to use these services to share their experience with people back on Earth. Some of the most popular, including Chris Hadfield and Scott Kelly, have amassed millions of followers each. Kelly lived on the ISS for nearly a full year in 2015–2016. From his Twitter account, he shared hundreds of images of landscapes, city lights, and daily life inside the station.

The astronauts cannot post directly to the social media sites themselves. Instead, they take photos and send them to NASA's social media team on the ground. The team figures out when and how to post it and then puts it online. NASA sees social media as a powerful way to share photos and videos of its missions with the public. Astronaut Reid Weisman notes, "Imagine if Neil Armstrong and Buzz Aldrin had had social media when they were on the moon. It would be a totally different experience for everybody."[3]

Scott Kelly setting up camera equipment aboard the ISS, 2015

Challenges of Orbital Photography

Taking photos in low-Earth orbit can be a challenge. One of the biggest hurdles is how fast the station is moving. Since it circles the globe at approximately 17,500 miles per hour (27,000 kmh), features on the ground below can quickly pass out of view. Astronauts may have as little as ten seconds in which to get the photo they want.

To maximize the chances of getting the desired photos, the cameras in the Cupola are turned on all the time. The lens caps are usually left off, and each camera is fitted with a different type of lens. Some provide a zoomed-in view, while others give a wider perspective. There is no time to switch lenses, so astronauts typically pick up a camera, shoot a few images, then reach for another camera and repeat.

The lighting conditions in space can also be difficult to deal with, especially when photographing the ISS or another spacecraft. Above Earth's atmosphere, the sun is much

IMPROVISING ON THE ISS

Astronaut Don Pettit is one of NASA's top experts on space photos. A photography hobbyist since childhood, he sought to take the best possible images while on the ISS. One of the major problems he faced was the speed of the ISS orbit. As the Earth moves past below, photos with a long exposure time can become blurred. During his first flight on the ISS in 2003, Pettit used spare parts he found around the station to build a simple device called a barn door tracker. It allows the camera to slowly turn during a shot to match the motion of Earth. The result is a much clearer photo than would otherwise be possible.

brighter and shadows are much darker. Without air to reflect and scatter light, the shadows are not partially filled in, as they often are on Earth. Instead, objects are either brightly lit or extremely dark. Astronauts must learn how to adjust the camera settings to take good photos in these conditions.

The lack of atmosphere may make things difficult for astronaut photographers, but it is a huge advantage for space-based telescopes. Without clouds or haze in the way, these observatories can see sharp views of objects in our solar system and far beyond. The most successful of them, delivered to orbit by the space shuttle in 1990, is the Hubble Space Telescope.

CHAPTER SIX

Looking Deep into Space and Time

The project that became the Hubble Space Telescope was first proposed in 1969. After years of preliminary studies and designs, the US Congress approved the money for the telescope in 1977. The telescope became one of the planned cargoes for the space shuttle, which was then in development. By 1986, the telescope was built and named for pioneering American astronomer Edwin Hubble. It was slated for a launch in October of that year. However, the loss of the shuttle *Challenger* in January stopped flights for two years while

Story Musgrave installed covers to protect Hubble instruments in 1993.

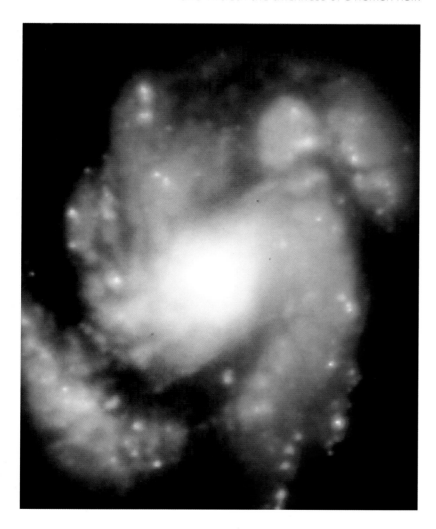

The flaw in Hubble's mirror was approximately one-fiftieth the thickness of a human hair.

NASA worked out the shuttle's problems. Hubble was put into storage, where its designers maintained and upgraded it. In April 1990, it finally reached Earth orbit aboard the space shuttle *Discovery*.

When Hubble's first images returned, scientists quickly realized there was a problem. The photos were distorted and out of focus. Hubble's main mirror had a flaw. Its shape was off only by a tiny fraction of an inch, but this was enough to blur the photos. The engineers

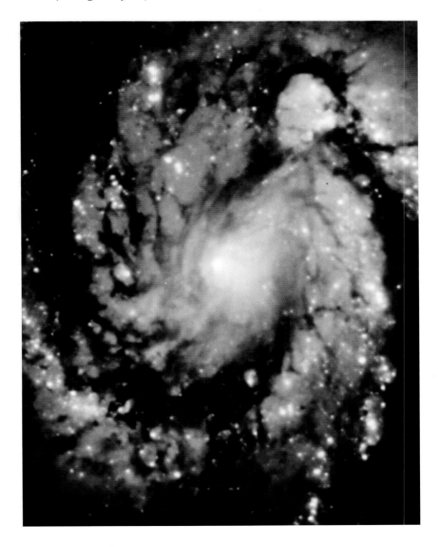

began working to find a solution. Luckily, they had designed Hubble to be visited and upgraded by astronauts aboard the space shuttle. NASA developed a device to correct the telescope's vision and prepared for a complex, risky repair mission.

The shuttle *Endeavour* arrived at Hubble in December 1993. Its seven-person crew began a grueling five-day sequence of spacewalks to fix the telescope. They added a corrective device called COSTAR

(Corrective Optics Space Telescope Axial Replacement) and performed other maintenance. Thanks to 11 months of training, the mission was a success. The first clear, sharp, post-repair images were released to the public in January 1994. Hubble scientists soon began amazing people around the world with the telescope's stunning, vivid photos of distant galaxies and nebulae.

The *Pillars of Creation*

One of Hubble's most famous photos was taken in 1995. It shows three dark columns of gas glowing in the light of nearby stars. The scene is from the Eagle Nebula, which is located approximately 6,500 light-years from Earth. Its appearance is typical of the areas in space where new stars form. Astronomer Paul Scowen, who led observations of the Eagle Nebula, noted, "Nebulous star-forming regions . . . are the interstellar neon signs that say, 'We just made a bunch of massive stars here.'"[3] The photo has been nicknamed the *Pillars of Creation*.

The *Pillars of Creation* has since become one of Hubble's best-known photos. It has been used in films, has appeared on T-shirts, and was even featured on a postage stamp. In 2014, Hubble revisited the Eagle Nebula with an upgraded camera. This time, astronomers photographed the area in infrared light in addition to visible light. The infrared light shines through the gas and dust of the pillars, revealing newly created stars within.

Hubble's 1995 and 2014 *Pillars of Creation* photos

M16 ▪ Eagle Nebula
Hubble Space Telescope ▪ WFPC2 ▪ WFC3/UVIS

The XDF combines ten years of Hubble photos and shows galaxies 13.2 billion years old. The universe is 13.7 billion years old.

The Deep Fields

When Hubble looks at extremely distant objects, it is looking at the light that left them billions of years in the past. Such objects are extremely faint when viewed from Earth. But Hubble is able to focus on a single area for a long period of time, collecting enough light to make these faraway things visible. This is the goal of Hubble's deep field photographs.

In January 1996, NASA released the first of its deep field photos. Assembled from 342 photographs taken over ten days, the image represents an area of sky equivalent to the width of a dime

located 75 feet (23 m) away. This spot, which appears through a normal telescope as mostly

dark, contained more than 1,500 galaxies. Some of them date back billions of years into the early

universe.[4]

NASA followed up this effort with 2004's Ultra Deep Field. It showed thousands of galaxies

in this small area. In 2012, the eXtreme Deep Field (XDF) photo took this even further, examining

a tiny patch of sky within the Ultra Deep Field with more sensitivity. Approximately 5,500

galaxies appeared in the photo. Astronomer Garth Illingworth explained, "The XDF is the

deepest image of the sky ever obtained and

reveals the faintest and most distant galaxies

ever seen. XDF allows us to explore further back

in time than ever before."[5]

COMPETING FOR HUBBLE

Hubble's unique capabilities make it a desirable tool for astronomers around the world. The Space Telescope Science Institute reviews research proposals to ensure only the projects most suited to Hubble are chosen. Of more than 1,000 proposals received each year, approximately 200 are approved.[6] Once a study is approved, it must be scheduled. Each observation is scheduled down to the second.

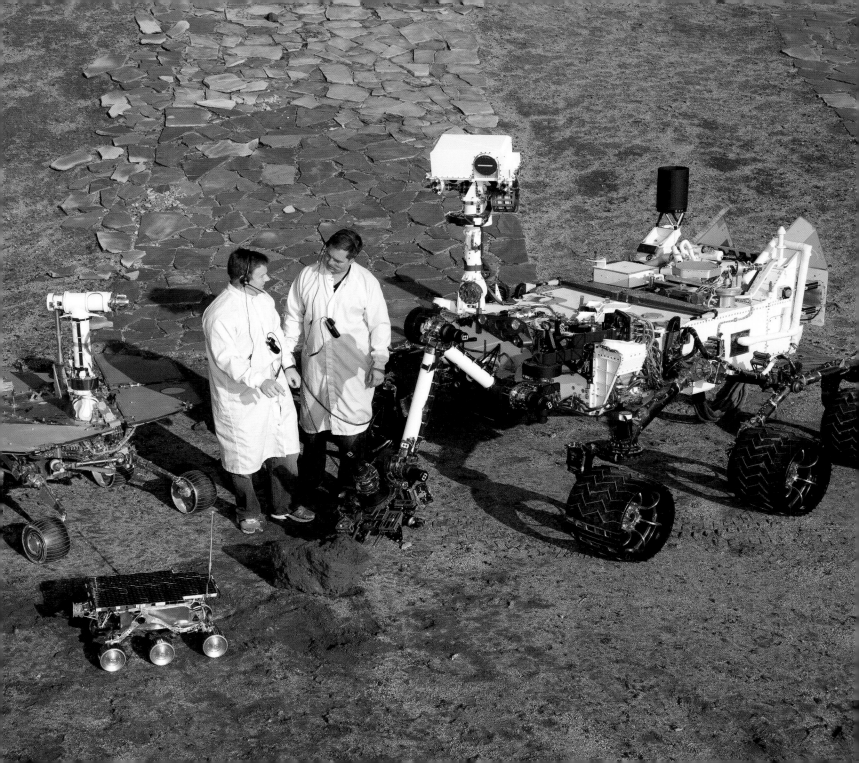

CHAPTER SEVEN

Mars in High Definition

Since December 1972, when the crew of *Apollo 17* blasted off from the surface of the moon and returned to Earth, no human has flown beyond low-Earth orbit. NASA hopes to change this in the coming decades. The agency has stated that one of its major upcoming goals is a human landing on Mars. The *Viking* spacecraft of the 1970s made important discoveries about the red planet, but more exploration would need to be done to pave the way for a landing. A series of rovers were central to these efforts.

Engineers in California show three generations of test versions of Mars rovers, *Sojourner, front, Spirit/Opportunity, left,* and *Curiosity, right.*

Spirit's microscopic imager took this photo of a Martian rock showing lava formations shaped by wind.

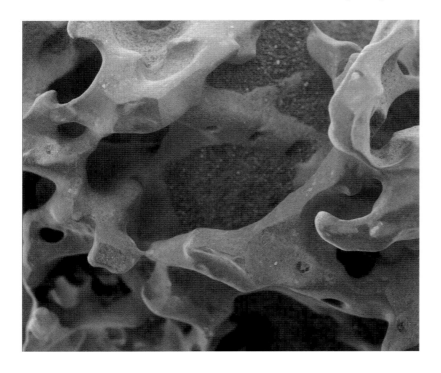

The *Sojourner* rover, roughly the size of a large remote-controlled car, arrived on Mars in 1997 and explored the area around its landing site for three months. It was followed in 2004 by twin golf cart–sized rovers named *Spirit* and *Opportunity*. The rovers, designed to operate for 90 days on the Martian surface, were stunning successes, continuing to work for years. Along the way, these rovers took thousands of photos and returned them to Earth, teaching scientists more about Martian geology, topography, and weather.

Curiosity's Cameras

On August 6, 2012, the largest and most sophisticated rover yet touched down inside Mars's Gale Crater. *Curiosity*, the size of a compact car, was equipped with a suite of scientific equipment to study Mars and determine whether life was once present on the planet. Among its tools were a total of 17 cameras—the most of any exploration spacecraft to date.[1]

The first of *Curiosity*'s cameras to begin shooting was the Mars Descent Imager (MARDI). Attached to the underside of the rover in a fixed position, MARDI took four color photos per second during the final two minutes of *Curiosity*'s fall through the thin Martian atmosphere. Once the rover settled on the surface, MARDI's mission was over. The camera's purpose was to help NASA determine precisely where the rover landed. As it neared the surface and got better images than any Mars orbiter, MARDI also helped mission planners make decisions about what nearby areas to explore first.

The rover's main structure was packed with eight black-and-white cameras designed to help the rover avoid hazards while driving, affectionately called the hazcams. Two pairs of hazcams point forward, and two pairs point backward. Each pair works together to generate

CAPTURING *CURIOSITY*'S LANDING

When *Curiosity* touched down in August 2012, another NASA spacecraft was already in orbit around Mars. The Mars Reconnaissance Orbiter (MRO), launched in 2005, had been mapping the red planet in high resolution for several years. When *Curiosity* approached Mars, NASA realized it had a unique opportunity to take a photo of the rover as it descended. As *Curiosity* fell to the Martian surface under its enormous parachute, the MRO flew overhead.

Signals from Earth to the rover, traveling at the speed of light, can take more than 20 minutes to arrive at Mars. The MRO's engineers commanded one of the orbiter's cameras to target the expected position of the rover, then hoped their calculations were correct. When the image was taken and sent back to Earth, it showed clearly the rover dangling below its parachute as it made its way through the thin Martian atmosphere.

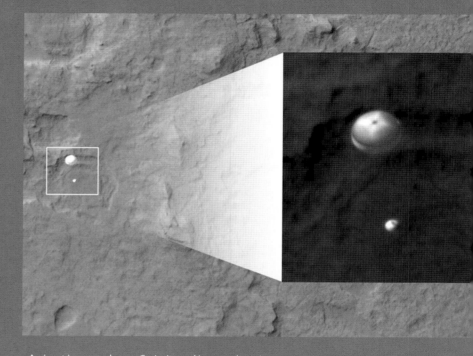

An inset image enlarges *Curiosity* and its parachute in this MRO photo.

a three-dimensional image of the nearby landscape. The rover is programmed to use the information from these cameras to avoid risky areas on its own.

Curiosity's mast contains another seven cameras. Four are navigation cameras, or navcams. Similar to the hazcams, these black-and-white cameras are arranged in pairs to create three-dimensional photos. They provide additional information to help the rover avoid obstacles. Also on the mast are two color cameras, called the mastcams. One is equipped with a zoom lens to see distant objects more clearly. The mastcams are useful for studying the texture, structure, and weathering of rocks Curiosity encounters. Scientists can also use them to analyze Martian weather events, such as dust storms. Besides taking still photos, the mastcams are capable of capturing high-definition video at ten frames per second.

An unretouched image from Curiosity's front left hazcam

The seventh camera on the rover's mast is the remote microimager. It works alongside a scientific instrument known as the laser-induced breakdown spectrometer (LIBS). LIBS fires a small laser at a nearby rock, then analyzes the vaporized rock material to determine what elements are inside. The job of the remote microimager is to take a photo of the rock before and after the laser strike. This helps scientists put the data from LIBS into context.

MARTIAN MEGAPIXELS

MAHLI and the mastcams all use the same digital camera sensors. Each sensor produces images with two million pixels, or two megapixels. By comparison, most smartphones available at the time *Curiosity* landed featured image sensors of eight megapixels or more. Why are the cameras on a multimillion-dollar rover not as good as the ones on a device that costs only a few hundred dollars? Spacecraft take several years to develop, and *Curiosity*'s cameras were selected in 2004. At that time, a two-megapixel sensor did not seem quite so old-fashioned. Additionally, the camera had to be simple, dependable, and able to survive months in space and years on Mars. The sensor NASA chose fit all these requirements. Finally, the rover team is able to take multiple photos and stitch them together into larger images. This makes having a single high-resolution camera unnecessary.

Curiosity's final camera is mounted at the end of its robotic arm. It is the Mars hand lens imager (MAHLI). A hand lens is a type of small magnifying glass geologists often bring into the field to study fine details of rocks. MAHLI's goal is to take photos on this same scale, giving scientists the kind of close-up looks at Martian rocks they might hope for if they were on the surface themselves. Small sensors protrude from the camera to ensure it does not come into contact with the rocks it is studying.

MAHLI is a versatile camera that is used for more than just looking at rocks. The robotic arm can be moved around to take images of the rover itself in order to diagnose any problems *Curiosity* is having. The arm can also be raised high into the air, above the view of any of the other cameras, for a taller perspective on the surroundings. Lights mounted on the camera, designed for taking nighttime photos, can also be used to let MAHLI see into holes drilled by the rover's other instruments.

Through 2016, both *Opportunity* and *Curiosity* were still actively exploring. The images and other data they returned to Earth taught scientists a great deal about Mars. They also helped pave the way for future human exploration of the red planet.

Selfies on Mars

The *Curiosity* rover team knew it could stitch together frames from MAHLI to generate large panoramic photos. Then, the team hit upon the idea of using this capability to take a self-portrait. It would not be easy. A self-portrait would require a carefully designed series of robotic arm motions. The camera would have to be moved to specific points in space to collect the frames. Along the way, the timing and motion of the arm would have to be planned to avoid its shadow getting into the photos.

Rather than testing these maneuvers on the real rover, the team used an identical rover back on Earth to rehearse the photos. It worked. On October 31, 2012, the team commanded the *Curiosity* rover to take its first complete self-portrait on Mars. It was made up of 55 individual frames combined into a single image.[2] Over the next few years, it took several more of these selfies. In addition to being interesting images, these photos also serve a practical purpose. They let mission planners track the condition of *Curiosity* over time as it travels across the dusty Martian surface.

A *Curiosity* self-portrait, compiled from images taken on May 11, 2016

CHAPTER EIGHT

Into the Outer Solar System

In the early 2000s, a new wave of robotic explorers investigated beyond Mars and into the deeper regions of the solar system. These probes broadened humanity's knowledge of gas giants, asteroids, and dwarf planets. Their cameras returned dramatically clearer images of these celestial bodies than had ever been seen before.

The *Cassini* spacecraft, launched in 1997, reached Saturn in 2004. The probe entered orbit around the ringed planet and began more than a decade of studying Saturn and its dozens of moons. It also dropped off a small lander, *Huygens*, which parachuted to the surface

The lander *Huygens* took these images as it descended to the surface of Saturn's moon Titan.

Cassini's image of backlit Saturn

of the moon Titan. *Cassini*'s cameras would give scientists their best views yet of the Saturnine system. Dr. Carolyn Porco leads *Cassini*'s imaging team. She says, "We are the eyes of *Cassini*. Our cameras capture all the dramatic sights and vistas there are to see around Saturn. And

through their imagery, they convey a sense of adventure, a sense of 'being there,' that we could otherwise only imagine."[1] *Cassini*'s imaging science system is the tool through which Porco and her team view Saturn. It includes one narrow-angle camera and one wide-angle camera.

Recalling the power of the *Pale Blue Dot* photo, Porco sought to use *Cassini* to create a similar image. To inspire the public, she spearheaded a social media campaign for people around the world to look up at the sky and smile and wave at Saturn during a 15-minute window on July 19, 2013. At this time, *Cassini* took 141 images with the probe's wide-angle camera. The team processed them into a stunning mosaic showing a backlit Saturn along with Earth, Venus, and Mars. On that day, the sun was blocked out behind Saturn, meaning *Cassini* could safely point its cameras back toward the inner solar system. Porco noted, "In this one magnificent view, Cassini has delivered to us a universe of marvels. And it did so on a day people all over the world, in unison, smiled in celebration at the sheer joy of being alive on a pale blue dot."[2]

THE MOST DISTANT SURFACE

The *Huygens* lander descended through Titan's thick atmosphere using a parachute. It came to rest safely on a rocky, icy plain. This was history's first landing in the outer solar system. With only a few hours of battery power, *Huygens* quickly took observations and relayed them to *Cassini*. Among these observations were photos of the landing site. The images are the most distant photos ever taken from the surface of a body in the solar system.

Pluto Revealed

In February 1930, US astronomer Clyde Tombaugh discovered Pluto. This tiny world lies far beyond the orbit of Neptune, the huge blue planet previously thought to be the solar system's most distant major body. From telescopes on Earth, Pluto appears as not much more than a point of light. Even using the Hubble Space Telescope in the early 2000s, the best photo of Pluto showed a blurry world with vaguely lighter and darker regions. A cutting-edge NASA space probe, *New Horizons*, would soon change this.

New Horizons launched from Florida in 2006. Its departure speed was faster than that of any other spacecraft in history. For nine years, the small probe coasted outward,

The rocks *Huygens* photographed on Titan's surface are believed to be made of water ice.

using Jupiter's powerful gravity to slingshot it into the solar system's outer reaches. Its high speed made it possible to reach Pluto in less than a decade, but that speed also made it impossible to slow down and orbit Pluto. *New Horizons* would have just one chance to observe the world as it zoomed past. The closest approach would come in July 2015.

The *New Horizons* spacecraft features three different cameras. Two are named Alice and Ralph, after characters from the 1950s television show *The Honeymooners*. Alice is able to both take images and detect which elements are present. It would be used to study the composition of Pluto's atmosphere. Ralph serves as the main observation platform for the spacecraft. It incorporates a group of black-and-white and color sensors, all of which use the same lens. It would be able to create maps of Pluto's surface with a resolution of approximately 820 feet (250 m) per pixel. Ralph would also help scientists improve their estimates of the exact sizes of Pluto and its moons.[3]

The spacecraft's third camera is the Long Range Reconnaissance Imager (LORRI). It features a large telescope to take close-up views at long distances. Approximately 180 days before the Pluto encounter, LORRI began taking images of Pluto and its moons. At this point, it saw only

PLUTO'S HEART

In the days leading up to *New Horizons*'s closest approach to Pluto, LORRI began sending back ever-clearer images of the world. One surface feature, captured in a July 7 photo, captured the imaginations of people around the world. A huge, heart-shaped basin covered a large swath of Pluto's surface. News articles and social media posters quickly seized upon the unusual sight, calling it Pluto's heart. Even NASA began referring to it this way.

The feature is approximately 1,000 miles (1,600 km) across at its widest point. As the spacecraft got closer to Pluto, it got better photos of the heart's surface. The region is nearly craterless, suggesting that it is relatively young geologically. It contains icy plains crisscrossed by hills and troughs, with occasional sections of pitted surfaces. Scientists suspected the cracked plains may have been formed by the contraction of the surface. Another theory suggested that the features may have been caused by heat within the dwarf planet interacting with the frozen surface. The *New Horizons* team named this region Tombaugh Regio, honoring the astronomer who discovered Pluto more than 80 years before.

Pluto's heart

dots of light. As *New Horizons* streaked toward its target, Pluto grew bigger in LORRI's view each day. At 60 days out, LORRI's photos were clearer than any taken by Hubble. From this point until the encounter, every subsequent image it took would be the best image of Pluto ever seen. At the closest approach, LORRI would be able to take photos with a resolution of approximately 160 feet (50 m).[4]

On July 15, *New Horizons* flew within 7,800 miles (12,600 km) of Pluto. The spacecraft rapidly carried out a preprogrammed sequence of photos and other observations. Getting all of this data back took time. At such a vast distance from Earth, the signal from the spacecraft was very faint. The last of the data from the encounter reached scientists on Earth in October 2016. However, the first few images from the encounter arrived within days. They showed a strange, complex world covered in icy mountain ranges, massive faults, and broad, smooth basins. The data streaming back from *New Horizons*'s cameras would keep scientists busy for years to come.

Seeing Outer Space

From the first tentative peeks above the atmosphere in the 1940s to today's exploration of the outer solar system, photography has allowed people everywhere to join humanity's journeys into space. Along the way, NASA's astronauts and robotic probes have created some of history's most iconic photos. Some are exotic vistas from faraway planets or moons. Others are glimpses back at Earth from afar. All of these images help to frame humanity's place in the universe.

Though most people cannot yet travel into space, photography makes it possible to share the sense of exploration. In the case of NASA, it also allows the taxpayers who are ultimately funding these voyages to see their money at work. Astronaut Don Pettit notes that the efforts of NASA echo those of past expeditions into the unknown: "Explorers [have always taken] pictures and always shared the adventures with people that stayed back home. We are doing the same thing."[5]

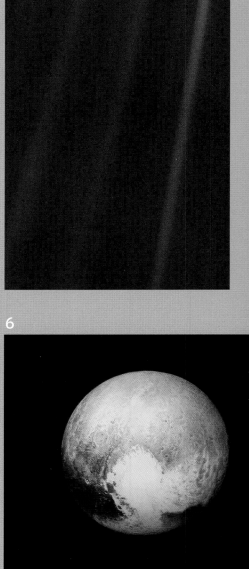

PHOTOGRAPHING SPACE

1. **V-2 photo from space**

   A camera on a V-2 rocket took the first photo from above the atmosphere in 1946. The image realized a dream of humanity—viewing Earth from outside the planet itself.

2. *Earthrise*

   The Apollo 8 astronauts took iconic photos of Earth rising over the lunar horizon from the moon's orbit in December 1968.

3. *Pale Blue Dot*

   On its way out of the solar system, *Voyager 1* turned back toward the sun to photograph the inner planets. Among the images it took is a photo of Earth as a tiny blue point of light.

4. Hubble's *Pillars of Creation*

   After astronauts repaired it, the Hubble Space Telescope began taking vivid photos of distant galaxies and nebulae. One image, dubbed the *Pillars of Creation*, shows tall, dark columns of gas in which new stars are being born.

5. *Curiosity* rover selfie

   Curiosity's robotic arm allows the rover to take photos from different angles that can be stitched together into a self-portrait.

6. *New Horizons* Pluto "heart" photo

   The *New Horizons* probe captured a series of stunning close-up photos of Pluto. One of the early photos sent back showed a distinct heart-like feature.

Quote

"There is perhaps no better demonstration of the folly of human conceits than this distant image of our tiny world. To me, it underscores our responsibility to . . . preserve and cherish the pale blue dot, the only home we've ever known."

—*Carl Sagan on* Voyager 1*'s* Pale Blue Dot *photo*

GLOSSARY

exposure
The setting on a camera that determines how much light reaches the film or sensor.

focus
The setting on a camera that adjusts the lens in a way that lets it produce clear images of objects at various differences.

gas giant
A large planet composed mainly of gaseous hydrogen and helium.

infrared
Light with longer wavelengths than are visible to human eyes.

nebula
A cloud of gas or dust in space.

negative
The reverse of an image that appears on a glass plate or film when it is exposed to light.

orbit
An elliptical path around a body in space.

panorama
A wide photo.

pixel

A tiny dot that makes up a single element of a digital image.

probe

A spacecraft designed to explore and transmit data about its findings.

reconnaissance

An exploration of an area to gather information.

rendezvous

The meeting of two objects in orbit.

rover

A wheeled robotic vehicle that explores a planet or moon and returns data to Earth.

spectrometer

A device that analyzes wavelengths of light to determine what elements are present.

viewfinder

A window in a camera through which the photographer can look to frame a shot.

ADDITIONAL RESOURCES

Selected Bibliography

"Astronaut Still Photography During Apollo." *NASA History Program Office*. NASA, 28 Jan. 2016. Web. 17 May 2016.

Poole, Robert. Earthrise*: How Man First Saw the Earth*. New Haven, CT: Yale UP, 2008. Print.

Reichhardt, Tony. "First Photo from Space." *Air & Space*. Smithsonian, Nov. 2006. Web. 17 May 2016.

Further Readings

Kruesi, Liz. *Astronomy*. Minneapolis: Abdo, 2016. Print.

Kruesi, Liz. *Space Exploration*. Minneapolis: Abdo, 2016. Print.

Nataraj, Nirmala. *Earth and Space: Photographs from the Archives of NASA*. San Francisco, CA: Chronicle, 2015. Print.

Websites

To learn more about Defining Images, visit **abdobooklinks.com**. These links are routinely monitored and updated to provide the most current information available.

For More Information

For more information on this subject, contact or visit the following organizations:

SMITHSONIAN NATIONAL AIR AND SPACE MUSEUM

Independence Ave at 6th Street, SW
Washington, DC 20560
202-633-2214
https://airandspace.si.edu/

The National Air and Space Museum features artifacts from throughout NASA's history, including capsules from the Mercury, Gemini, and Apollo Programs, as well as the space shuttle *Discovery*.

KANSAS COSMOSPHERE

1100 N Plum St
Hutchinson, KS 67501
800-397-0330
http://cosmo.org/

The Kansas Cosmosphere displays a wide variety of space artifacts, including several cameras flown during the Apollo Program.

SOURCE NOTES

CHAPTER 1. *EARTHRISE*

1. Robert Poole. Earthrise: *How Man First Saw the Earth*. New Haven, CT: Yale UP, 2008. Print. 1.

2. Ibid. 2.

3. "Astronaut Still Photography During Apollo." *NASA History Program Office*. NASA, 28 Jan. 2016. Web. 7 Dec. 2016.

4. Robert Poole. Earthrise: *How Man First Saw the Earth*. New Haven, CT: Yale UP, 2008. Print. 24.

5. Ibid. 28.

CHAPTER 2. SPACE COMES INTO FOCUS

1. Robert Poole. Earthrise: *How Man First Saw the Earth*. New Haven, CT: Yale UP, 2008. Print. 53.

2. Ibid. 53.

3. Ibid. 50.

4. "Rocket and Missile System: Strategic Missiles." *Encyclopedia Britannica*. Encyclopedia Britannica, 3 Feb. 2012. Web. 7 Dec. 2016.

5. Tony Reichhardt. "First Photo from Space." *Air & Space*. Smithsonian Institution, 24 Oct. 2006. Web. 7 Dec. 2016.

6. Robert Poole. Earthrise: *How Man First Saw the Earth*. New Haven, CT: Yale UP, 2008. Print. 70.

7. Ibid. 64.

8. Ibid. 67.

9. "NASA Johnson Space Center Oral History Project Edited Oral History Transcript: Richard W. Underwood." *NASA Johnson Space Center*, 17 Oct. 2000. Web. 7 Dec. 2016.

CHAPTER 3. PHOTOS FROM THE MOON

1. Doug Bierend. "The Hackers Who Recovered NASA's Lost Lunar Photos." *Wired.* Condé Nast, 23 Apr. 2014. Web. 7 Dec. 2016.

2. Albert J. Derr. "Photography Equipment and Techniques: A Survey of NASA Developments." *NASA.* NASA, 1972. Web. 7 Dec. 2016.

3. Robert Poole. Earthrise: *How Man First Saw the Earth.* New Haven, CT: Yale UP, 2008. Print. 93.

4. "NASA Spacecraft Images Offer Sharper Views of Apollo Landing Sites." *NASA.* NASA, 5 Sept. 2011. Web. 7 Dec. 2016.

CHAPTER 4. VOYAGING TO THE PLANETS

1. Edward A. Guinness. "Archive of Viking Lander 1 and 2 EDR Images." *pdsimage.wr.usgs. gov.* McDonnell Center for the Space Sciences, n.d. Web. 7 Dec. 2016.

2. "The Golden Record." *Voyager: The Interstellar Mission.* Jet Propulsion Laboratory, California Institute of Technology, n.d. Web. 7 Dec. 2016.

3. Carl Sagan. *Pale Blue Dot: A Vision of the Human Future in Space.* New York: Random, 1994. Print. 7.

4. Ibid. 9.

CHAPTER 5. TURNING THE CAMERA BACK TOWARD EARTH

1. "Missions: Space Shuttle." *NASA*. NASA, n.d. Web. 7 Dec. 2016.

2. Clara Moskowitz. "Shutterbug Astronauts Smash Space Photography Record." *Space*. Space, 2 Apr. 2010. Web. 7 Dec. 2016.

3. Laurie Vazquez. "How NASA Turned Astronauts into Social Media Superstars." *Popular Science*. Popular Science, 9 Oct. 2015. Web. 7 Dec. 2016.

CHAPTER 6. LOOKING DEEP INTO SPACE AND TIME

1. Brian Handwerk. "Hubble Telescope at 20: NASA Astronomers' Top Photos." *National Geographic*. National Geographic, 26 Apr. 2010. Web. 7 Dec. 2016.

2. Francie Diep. "How the Hubble Space Telescope's Iconic Photos Changed the Way Everybody Saw Space." *Pacific Standard*. Pacific Standard, 24 Apr. 2015. Web. 7 Dec. 2016.

3. "Hubble Goes High-Definition to Revisit Iconic 'Pillars of Creation.'" *NASA*. NASA, 5 Jan. 2015. Web. 7 Dec. 2016.

4. "Hubble's Deepest View of the Universe Unveils Bewildering Galaxies across Billions of Years." *Hubblesite*. NASA, 15 Jan. 1996. Web. 7 Dec. 2016.

5. "Hubble Goes to the eXtreme to Assemble Farthest-Ever View of the Universe." *NASA*. NASA, 25 Sept. 2012. Web. 7 Dec. 2016.

6. "The Telescope: Team Hubble." *Hubblesite*. NASA, n.d. Web. 7 Dec. 2016.

CHAPTER 7. MARS IN HIGH DEFINITION

1. "Curiosity's Cameras." *NASA Podcasts*. NASA, 13 June 2013. Web. 7 Dec. 2016.

2. Emily Lakdawalla. "The Story behind Curiosity's Self-Portrait." *The Planetary Society*. The Planetary Society, 19 Aug. 2015. Web. 7 Dec. 2016.

CHAPTER 8. INTO THE OUTER SOLAR SYSTEM

1. "Inside the Spacecraft." *Cassini Solstice Mission*. Jet Propulsion Laboratory, California Institute of Technology, n.d. Web. 7 Dec. 2016.

2. "NASA *Cassini* Spacecraft Provides New View of Saturn and Earth." *NASA*. NASA, 12 Nov. 2013. Web. 7 Dec. 2016.

3. "Spacecraft: Payload." *New Horizons: NASA's Mission to Pluto*. Johns Hopkins Applied Physics Laboratory, 2016. Web. 7 Dec. 2016.

4. Ibid.

5. Mia Tramz. "A Master Class in Space Photography with NASA Astronaut Donald Pettit." *Time*. Time, 17 July 2014. Web. 7 Dec. 2016.

INDEX

About the Author

Arnold Ringstad has written more than 50 books for audiences ranging from kindergarteners to high-schoolers. He has also published research in the *Journal of Cold War Studies*. He is an avid reader of books about history and space exploration. Ringstad graduated from the University of Minnesota in 2011. He resides in Minnesota.